Muay Thai

Thai boxing

'Highly recommended reading for
any aspiring martial artist.
This series will enhance your
knowledge of styles, history,
grading systems and finding and
analyzing the right club.'

Stan 'The Man' Longinidis
8-times World Kickboxing
Champion

PAUL COLLINS

In memory of Dana Goodson—a big loss to Australian kickboxing.

This edition first published in 2002 in the United States of America by
Chelsea House Publishers, a subsidiary of Haights Cross Communications.

Chelsea House Publishers
1974 Sproul Road, Suite 400
Broomall, PA 19008-0914

The Chelsea House world wide web address is www.chelseahouse.com

Library of Congress Cataloging-in-Publication Data Applied for.

ISBN 0-7910-6870-6

First published in 2002 by
MACMILLAN EDUCATION AUSTRALIA PTY LTD
627 Chapel Street, South Yarra, Australia 3141

Text design and page layout by Judith Summerfeldt Grace and
  Kae Goodsell-Sato
Cover design by Judith Summerfeldt Grace
Illustration on page 9 by Kae Goodsell-Sato
Edited by Carmel Heron

Printed in China

Acknowledgments
Photographs by Nick Sandalis except pp. 10, 11, 30 courtesy of
Stewart Clarke and p. 8 courtesy of Getty Images.
The author would like to thank: Dr Peter Lewis, Director of the Malvern
Martial Arts Centre, 1291 Malvern Road, Malvern Vic, 3144, Australia;
Liam Robinson, WKA British Muay Thai Boxing Champion (UK);
Sandy Remiens (NZ).

**Techniques used in this book should only be practiced
under qualified supervision.**

Contents

What are martial arts?

The main martial arts

Aikido (Japan)

Hapkido (Korea)

Judo (Japan)

Jujitsu (Japan)

Karate (Japan)

Kendo (Japan)

Kickboxing (USA)

Kung fu (China)

Muay Thai (Thailand)

Ninjutsu (Japan)

Samurai (Japan)

Sumo wrestling (Japan)

Taekwondo (Korea)

Tai chi (China)

Most people have seen at least one fantastic martial arts movie. A lot of it is trick photography. A **ninja** cannot really jump backwards and land on the roof of a towering house! Then again, martial arts are about belief—belief in yourself and your ability to overcome any obstacle, no matter how big or small.

Ask any martial arts student why they train and the answer will be to learn **self-defense**. But that answer only scratches the surface of the term 'martial arts'.

One of the many functions of martial arts is to train students, both physically and mentally.

Martial arts have ancient traditions steeped in discipline and dedication. Most martial arts have developed from ancient Asian combat skills. In **feudal** times, people in Asia had to defend themselves against attack. Quite often, peasants were not allowed to carry weapons, so self-defense became their weapon.

Some martial arts are fighting sports, such as karate and Muay Thai. Other martial arts, like tai chi, concentrate on self-improvement, although self-defense is part of the training.

Kendo

Karate

Ninjutsu

Dedication and discipline

Muay Thai is hard work. Ask any senior student. On average, it takes three years before a student of Muay Thai is good enough to fight in the ring. And then the *real* hard work begins.

Dedication plays a major role in the life of any martial arts student. Training sessions for the serious Muay Thai student can be twice a day, six days a week. Some students in Thailand dedicate their lives to the sport. A less dedicated student will train two times a week, on average. A session lasts from 60 to 90 minutes.

Students practice one simple procedure over and over again. They might repeat a simple move 200 times in one session, only to repeat the same move the next time they train. Martial artists learn through repetition, so that even the most basic moves can be automatically performed when they are suddenly required.

Muay Thai

Understanding Muay Thai

Muay Thai can be considered a subset of kickboxing

'Muay' translated means 'fighting' or 'boxing'. Muay Thai is commonly referred to as Thai boxing, and sometimes mistakenly called kickboxing. Kickboxing originated when karate promoters wanted a full-contact sport using traditional boxing methods, plus all the techniques used in karate. They combined Muay Thai with karate and coined the phrase 'kickboxing'.

Today, Muay Thai can be considered a **subset** of kickboxing. Most kickboxing clubs recognize four sets of rules:

1 Full-contact karate
2 Freestyle (with leg kicks)
3 Oriental rules (with knees)
4 Muay Thai (with elbows).

The rules followed dictate the type of strikes allowed in each style of fight. Freestyle fights allow kicks to the legs, whereas full-contact karate allows kicks above the waist only. Fights with oriental rules allow knee strikes to the opponent's ribs and sometimes to the face. Muay Thai rules allow elbow strikes, whereas the other three sets of rules forbid them. Sometimes fighters can choose to fight using a mixture of rules.

Most martial arts have strict rules. Muay Thai students enjoy more flexibility. Almost everything is considered legal. Fighters are allowed to kick, punch, knee and elbow their opponents. Grappling with or kicking an opponent while they are down is forbidden. Groin strikes are not allowed in Muay Thai. Biting and head-butting are banned from all martial arts.

In Muay Thai, fighters are allowed to use their knees to ram the opponent's face, use their shins to slam into parts beneath the waist and use their elbows to strike the face. Muay Thai is possibly the most violent of the martial arts.

Like all martial arts, Muay Thai has a **philosophy** laid down by its founders. The philosophy usually strives to bring out only the good in students. The following 'demands' are taught to Muay Thai students:

⊙ train the body, mind and heart. Physical conditioning is pointless without developing concentration and dedication

⊙ show patience and persistence with yourself and others

⊙ show respect for your parents, teachers, community and yourself

⊙ be honest and courteous, and help others when you have the opportunity

⊙ approach all situations with **diligence** and self-confidence

⊙ contribute to unity and spirit of the Muay Thai brotherhood

⊙ use common sense and intelligence when in a bad situation

⊙ practicing good Muay Thai means resorting to fighting only as a last resort.

Roundhouse kick to the head

Thailand: the birthplace of Muay Thai

Population:	**61.4 million**
Language:	**Thai**
Currency:	**Baht**
Main religion:	**Buddhism**

The Kingdom of Thailand covers an area of 514,000 square kilometers (319,194 square miles). Thailand lies in the heart of South-East Asia, roughly halfway between India and China. It shares borders with Myanmar (formerly Burma) to the west and north, Laos to the north and northeast, Cambodia to the east and Malaysia to the south.

Buddhist statues

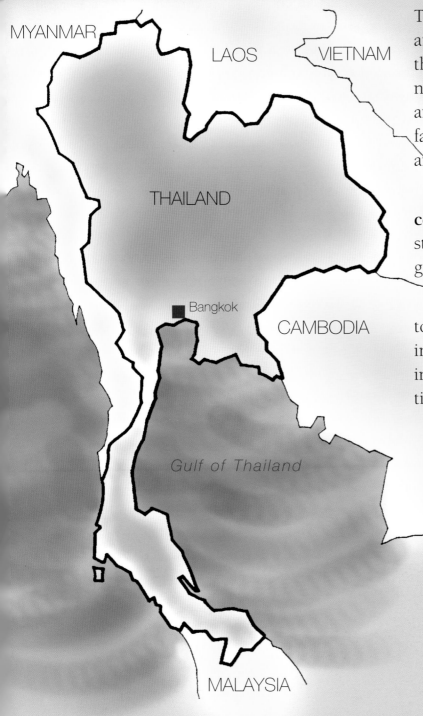

MYANMAR

LAOS

VIETNAM

THAILAND

■ Bangkok

CAMBODIA

Gulf of Thailand

MALAYSIA

Thailand is divided into four distinct areas: the north, which is mountainous; the Central Plains, which are fertile; the northeast, which is a **semi-arid plateau**; and the southern peninsula, which is famous for its beautiful tropical beaches and offshore islands.

The government of Thailand is a **constitutional monarchy**. The head of state is the King and the head of the government is the Prime Minister.

The southern peninsula is visited by tourists and the tourism industry is important to the Thai economy. Other industries include rice production, fishing, tin-mining and rubber production.

Thailand was known as Siam until 1939.

It's a fact!

The history of Muay Thai

Muay Thai sign in Patong, Phuket
(pronounced 'foo-ket')

Muay Thai can be traced back to Thailand around 1300 AD. No exact record exists because in 1769 Burmese armies destroyed Siam's capital, Ayutthaya, burning all documentation.

Muay Thai was originally a military combat style of fighting that complemented a soldier's sword and **pike** in close-range fighting.

A manual of warfare called the *Chupasart* was written and became the warrior's guide. It laid out theories on using knives, swords, spears, battle axes, pikes and cross bows without the actual weapons. There is no record of when the *Chupasart* first originated, but it is likely that it was started under the reign of King Ramathibodi II (1459–1529). New techniques were added to it when they were proven effective on the battlefield.

The *Chupasart* established how to use each body part as a weapon. The arms were defined as the twin swords of defense. The fist was the jabbing tip of a spear, and the elbow the battle axe to crush. The knee axed its way through and the foot was an arrow or knife. The shinbone became the staff of the pike, to block and strike.

The sport was once so violent that fighters' gloves were made from **hemp** soaked in glue with ground glass. Seashells and tree bark were used as groin guards against lethal kicks. It was only around 1927 that the famous Thai boxers Nai Kau Muangyos and Nai Nok Chai Sirisek wore western-style gloves.

The Thai government heavily sponsors this national sport. There are hundreds of training camps—so many, in fact, that most provinces have clubs or camps that are usually run by families.

Muay Thai is now the most popular sport in Thailand and has an increasing following around the world. This following is probably boosted by kickboxing, which is extremely popular in countries such as America and England. Enthusiasts hope that one day Muay Thai will become an Olympic sport.

King Naresuan made Muay Thai famous in 1560 AD. Captured by the Burmese in one of the many battles between Siam and Burma, the king was given a chance to show how good a fighter he was. He fought and won against Burma's top fighters and returned home a hero.

A fight in progress, Paton, Phuket

Muay Thai boxers receiving instructions from the referee before a fight

Dress code and etiquette

Dress code

Muay Thai students usually wear loose-fitting shorts and females also wear a T-shirt. The shorts are made from various fabrics, even silk.

Because Muay Thai is a full-contact sport, students wear gloves while **sparring** and fighting. When training on punching bags, students wear 'bag' gloves, which are a smaller and more compact version of the gloves worn while sparring or fighting. The larger gloves are thickly padded to avoid serious injury when hitting, while the smaller gloves are solidly packed to withstand hard training on the bags.

This student is wearing shorts, gloves and protective headgear and shin guards.

Etiquette

There are certain things that will not be tolerated in Muay Thai. Etiquette is really a matter of good attitude when it comes to your gym and those training around you. The following rules are generally accepted rules in the gym:

- sitting down is not permitted

- smoking, eating and drinking are not allowed

- it is considered disrespectful to talk while the trainer is speaking

- when entering the ring, fighters should show their respect to the judges by bowing to the four sides of the ring. The same formality is expected when a winner is announced

- students should bow when entering the gym and when approaching the trainer

- senior fighters should assist with coaching when the head trainer is absent

- students are expected to help with the general tidiness of the gym.

Before you start

Choosing a club

A look through the telephone book under the general heading 'Martial Arts' will show you where the nearest clubs are.

Muay Thai clubs have different methods of training and they teach their own versions of maneuvers. Many clubs teach both kickboxing and Muay Thai.

It is better to join a large club with many members. Try to join a club that has students about your own age. If not, you could always join with a friend. It is also wise to check if the club has recognized fighters. Some clubs have well-known identities attached to their name, however lesser-ranked instructors teach students.

If money is a consideration, phone around and compare costs. Some clubs charge a joining fee, while other clubs only charge per visit. Visitors normally do not pay, so it is a good idea to sit in on a session or two before joining a club.

It's a fact!

In Thailand most of the professional Muay Thai fighters begin training as early as six years of age.

Joining a martial arts club can be fun. Club members can sign up for competitions and travel interstate or even overseas to represent their club. Some clubs also organize weekend camps.

Clothing

It is not expensive to start Muay Thai. Your first few training sessions can be performed in a pair of shorts and a T-shirt.

The clothing and equipment required are:

⊙ hand wraps: these are strips of cloth about 5 centimeters (1.97 inches) wide. They should be long enough to go around your wrists and knuckles 12 times. Hand wraps are used to strengthen your wrists against the impact on bags and your opponent

⊙ bag gloves

⊙ Thai boxing shorts and shirt

⊙ ankle supports (optional)

⊙ 16-ounce sparring gloves

⊙ shin guards

⊙ groin protector

⊙ mouthpiece (your dentist can make you a mouthpiece)

⊙ headgear.

Clubs should have all the protective equipment you will need, like leg, arm and shin guards, although it is better to buy your own once you start to train seriously. Personal equipment can be kept in better condition and will fit better than the standard club equipment. Second-hand padded guards and even gloves can be bought at recycled equipment stores and through personal advertisements in newspapers. Garage sales are also a good source of second-hand martial arts equipment.

How to apply hand wraps

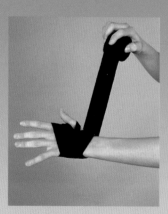

1 Loop hand wrap around the thumb

2 Wrap around the palm

3 Wrap around at the back of the thumb

4 Wrap around through the first knuckle

Insurance

Insurance is advised, although you are unlikely to get badly injured at a well-run martial arts school. Most clubs have insurance coverage so it pays to ask.

Did you know?

The Thai Ministry of Education has placed Muay Thai on the school curriculum. Muay Thai is also part of the Thai army's training. More recently it has been taught to the US SEAL teams, Special Forces, the CIA and the Secret Service.

Confidence and disabilities

Everyone feels nervous when they first enter a club. By the time you have kicked into the bag and perhaps sparred a few times, you will feel more confident.

A light stretching workout before competition is a good way to relax and to loosen stiff muscles. Good instructors will teach you breathing techniques, which will calm you and help you to focus.

A disability should not stop you from trying Muay Thai. Many top athletes have **asthma**. Other athletes have **diabetes**. Getting fit through Muay Thai can help improve your overall condition. Just make sure your instructor knows of your complaint, take the necessary precautions and bow out when you do not feel well.

⑤ *Take across top of the hand and behind the thumb*

⑥ *Repeat procedure with every finger and knuckle*

⑦ *Finish the wrap around the wrist and hold wrap in place with velcro*

Fitness and training

Practicing a front kick on a pad

Beginner martial artists are not usually ready for serious training. This takes time. They need to build fitness slowly. Most martial arts clubs have beginners' classes, where students learn the basic self-defense techniques and get fit.

At the start of each training session, students perform warm-up and stretching exercises. The instructor will then teach the class something new or ask them to practice on the bag or focus pads with a partner. Partner training teaches timing, reaction, balance, self-control and countering skills.

Sparring in the ring is sometimes part of a training session, and the instructor will usually choose two opponents of equal ability.

Training sessions are usually 90 minutes each. Unlike other martial arts, Muay Thai training includes skipping, weights, bag work and speed balls. Speed balls are football-sized leather balls attached to a board. Hitting the moving ball under the board helps teach rhythm and coordination.

Unlike all other martial arts, in Muay Thai boxers use skipping for fitness.

Stretching quads

Stretching hamstrings

Hip flex

Groin stretch

Stretching quads

Stretching

As well as fitness you will need to gain flexibility. This means stretching all your body parts. You need to loosen and warm tight and cold muscles.

It is important to keep each stretching movement gentle and slow. You should not use jerking or bouncing movements.

Stretching has many purposes. It:

◉ increases heart and lung capacity

◉ helps you practice movements you are about to perform

◉ helps avoid injury from pulled muscles

◉ gives you greater flexibility.

It is equally important to cool down after exercising. This maintains the level of blood circulation and reduces muscle spasms. Gentle cool-down stretches also help prevent injuries because they reduce muscle tightness.

Sparring

Because Muay Thai is a full-contact sport, students must learn how to take a hit as well as how to deliver one. Of all the martial artists, Muay Thai fighters are possibly the best conditioned. This is because their training is extremely hard, and their bodies have to withstand blows to almost every part of the body.

Shadow boxing is one form of sparring, and this is performed solo. Fighters practice leg work like roundhouse kicks and jab kicks, and hand work such as **uppercuts** and elbow strikes.

Sparring with a partner can be performed in the ring to help students become familiar with fighting in the ring. Students pair off and exchange techniques with each other, usually without the partner knowing the next move. Sparring is practiced in training and it is important as it teaches students which techniques will work in real-life situations, as well as in actual competitive fights.

Sparring sharpens reflexes and allows students to practice their technique.

Muay Thai techniques

There are many kicks, punches and strikes to learn in Muay Thai. You will find some easier to master than others. You will need to practice even the techniques that you do not like. Every technique has been developed over many years for a specific purpose.

Ground-grappling techniques, such as those used in judo or jujitsu, have not been developed for Muay Thai.

Did you know?

There is no belt system in Muay Thai. The skills and expertise of fighters are tested only in the ring against opponents. The only belts of concern to serious Muay Thai fighters are the championship belts of Lumphini Stadium and the Ratchadamnoen Stadium.

Punching techniques

Punches are normally delivered to either the face or the abdomen. Unlike other boxers, Muay Thai boxers often trap, or lock, their opponent's striking arm and counter attack. In *Kon Erawan Suey Nga*, the defender moves in close to their opponent and delivers a solid uppercut to the chin. This technique can easily end the fight with a knockout.

How to form a fist

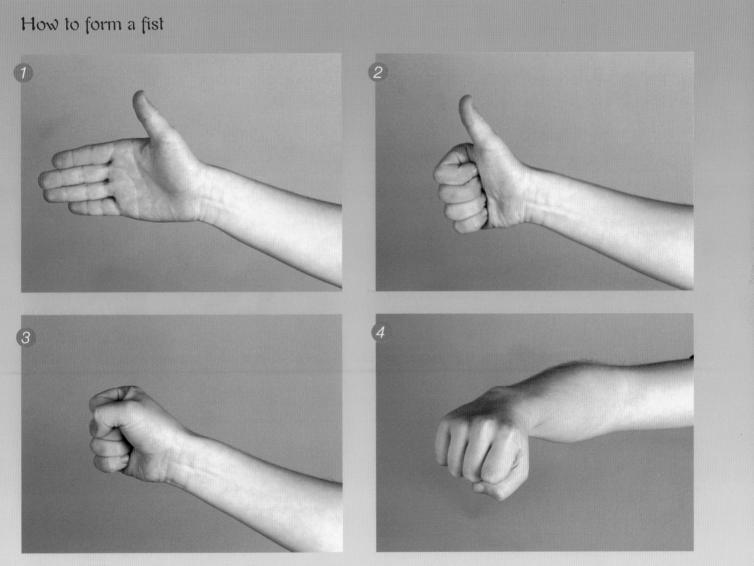

Fighters hit with the front two knuckles, which are the biggest and strongest.

Striking techniques

Elbow strikes

The elbow strike is one of the Thai fighter's most powerful weapons. Elbow strikes to the head are banned in all martial arts except Muay Thai. In Muay Thai, elbow strikes score high points and often result in knockouts.

Elbow strikes can be used when facing the opponent and when a fighter's back is turned. Elbow strikes are usually aimed at either the face or the abdomen, but can also be delivered to an opponent's back.

In *Sak Poung Ma-Lai*, the elbow is thrown into the opponent's ribs. This technique can be used when a defender has successfully sidestepped an attacker's punch or kick.

After successfully countering an attack by passing beneath a punch, a defender can move quickly behind their opponent and deliver an elbow strike to the attacker's back. This technique is called *Kon Sok Thay Thoy*.

Knee strikes

In close combat the knees are also a decisive weapon. Knee blows are dealt to the back, ribs, thighs, belly and, in a more spectacular fashion, to the head. The head can then be pulled down to meet the knee blow, a move called 'flying knees'. It is also an excellent counter to the 'wall of defense', which is a shielding technique using uplifted leg, elbows and forearms to guard against attack.

Practicing 'flying knees' on a pad

Knee strikes have to be delivered close in to your opponent because they lack the distance of the punch and the kick. Many knee strikes occur when Muay Thai fighters are locked, or grappling one another.

Flying knees: the head is pulled down to meet the knee blow

Knees are an important weapon in Muay Thai.

Kicking techniques

There are many kicks in Muay Thai, some of which are designed to annoy the opponent rather than cripple them. In *Vi Roon Hog Klab*, a kick to the soft flesh of the opponent is used to cause discomfort, hopefully making the opponent lose concentration and causing them to make mistakes.

One of the more famous aspects of the Thai fighter is the toughness of their shins. Thai fighters are trained to toughen their shins so that the nerves are conditioned to withstand pain. Shins are used like clubs, powered with driving force from the hips. A kick like this is so powerful that it is the favored kick in the majority of fights.

Kicks to the back of the knee will fell any opponent if executed correctly.

26

The jab kick is unique to Muay Thai and kickboxers.

Counter attack with a left roundhouse kick

In *Ten Kwad Larn*, a swift and sweeping low kick to the back of the opponent can have many effects. It can topple them if executed correctly, or can unbalance them just enough to leave themselves open to a more direct attack. This is called a combination attack—one attack is not sufficient so a follow-up technique is also delivered.

Perhaps the most common kick of all, the roundhouse kick is usually delivered to the opponent's head. Known as *Na Rai Ban Sean*, this kick has often knocked opponents out.

A little known kick outside of Muay Thai is the jab kick. It is usually a defensive kick to keep an opponent at bay but, when applied with precision and purpose, it can drop the strongest foe. It is especially useful when facing an opponent who is rushing toward you.

27

The language of Muay Thai

Most commands you hear in Muay Thai are spoken in Thai. It is a sign of respect to know Thai as this is where Muay Thai originated. A student can travel anywhere in the world and understand the language of Muay Thai.

Thai writing is not based on the English alphabet or sounds. There is no universally accepted way of translating the sounds into English letters. Therefore, all the translations that you see are individual writers' **phonetic approximations**. While travelling in Thailand, visitors will notice that cities are spelt differently on signs just kilometers apart.

To learn Muay Thai, you will need to know some of the following expressions. Some of the terms can vary from club to club.

andap	rating
bat	block
champ	champion
dtae	to kick
dtae kao	knee kick
dtae wiang	roundhouse kicking
dtee	to hit
dtoi	to box
dtoi lom	shadow boxing
gamagan	referee
garsawb	punching
gawn welaa	novice bout
hua	head
kai boxing	camp
kao	knee
kradot	jump

kradot dtae	jumping kick	
kru	instructor	
kwaa	right	
lop	to duck	
mat at	uppercut	
mat drong	straight punch	
muay sakon	international boxing	
na kaeng	shin	
nak muay	boxer	
nuam	gloves	
saai	left	
sawing	swing	
sawk or sok	elbow	
ting	throw	
weh tee	ring	
yaek	break	

Counting one to ten

nueng	one	1
song	two	2
sarm	three	3
see	four	4
ha	five	5
hok	six	6
dedt	seven	7
baedt	eight	8
kow	nine	9
sib	ten	10

Competition

The winner proudly displays his championship belt, which he has retained by winning.

The standard Muay Thai ring is 6 meters (20 feet) square. There are many officials, including three judges, a referee, a time keeper, a doctor and usually a score keeper or ringside supervisor.

A fight consists of five rounds, lasting three minutes each. There are two-minute rest periods between rounds. The most points per round a fighter can achieve are ten points. At the end of the five rounds the judges will add up the points and the fighter with the most points wins. If at the end of the five rounds both fighters have equal points, it is declared a draw.

If a fighter is unable to continue a fight after the referee counts to ten, then a 'knockout' is declared. If, in the opinion of the referee, one fighter can no longer fight without causing themselves serious injury, the referee will stop the fight and a technical knockout is declared.

If a fighter commits a serious **misdemeanor**, the referee can award the fight to the opponent.

The heaviest fighters are called superheavy and the lightest are called flyweight. Which weight division would you fight in?					
Superheavy	91.9 kilograms and above	(202.6 pounds and above)	Superwelter	66.9–69.5 kilograms	(147.5–153.2 pounds)
Heavyweight	88.3–91.8 kilograms	(194.7–202.4 pounds)	Welterweight	64.6–66.8 kilograms	(142.4–147.3 pounds)
Cruiserweight	84.7–88.2 kilograms	(186.7–194.4 pounds)	Lightwelter	62.4–64.5 kilograms	(137.6–142.2 pounds)
Lightcruiser	81.5–84.6 kilograms	(179.7–186.5 pounds)	Superlight	60.1–62.3 kilograms	(132.5–137.3 pounds)
Lightheavy	78.2–81.4 kilograms	(172.4–179.5 pounds)	Lightweight	58.3–60.0 kilograms	(128.5–132.3 pounds)
Supermiddle	75.1–78.1 kilograms	(165.6–172.2 pounds)	Featherweight	56.5–58.2 kilograms	(124.6–128.3 pounds)
Middleweight	72.4–75.0 kilograms	(159.8–165.3 pounds)	Bantamweight	54.6–56.4 kilograms	(120.4–124.3 pounds)
Lightmiddle	69.6–72.3 kilograms	(153.4–159.4 pounds)	Flyweight	53.3–54.5 kilograms	(117.5–120.2 pounds)

Glossary

asthma	a breathing disorder
Buddhism	a religion that started in Asia
constitutional monarchy	a country that has a king or queen who does not govern, rather they are a figurehead
diabetes	a disease where the body does not fully process sugar
diligence	good effort
feudal	dating back to the Middle Ages, when all the land was owned by the nobility and the peasants worked for them
hemp	native Asian herb that produces tough fibers used to manufacture rope and fabric
misdemeanor	a wrong act
ninja	traditionally a spy or assassin
philosophy	theory about the meaning of things
phonetic approximations	spelling something as it is pronounced
pike	weapon consisting of a long pole with a spike at the end
self-defense	usually grappling, which involves pinning your opponent so that they cannot strike you
semi-arid plateau	a high flat area with little rainfall
sparring	exchanging techniques with a partner
subset	a small part of a larger category
uppercuts	strikes that bring the fist up under an opponent's chin

Index